# CONTINENTAL
## *Cuisine*

Berryland
Books

Managing Editor: Richard Johnston
Author: Dr. Anita Shan
Designer: Prof. Madhu Krishna, Signet Designs, India.

Printed and bound in China
ISBN 1-84577-651-8

A catalogue record of this book is available from the British Library

NB: Recipes using uncooked eggs or meat or fish should be avoided by infants,
the elderly, pregnant women and anyone suffering from an illness.

# Contents

# Appetizers

## Skewered vegetables from Provence with herb sauce and baguette

### Serves 4

### Ingredients

- 16 small button mushrooms
- 1 yellow pepper
- 2 small courgettes
- 2 onions
- 16 cherry tomatoes
- 5 sprigs thyme
- 1 sprig rosemary
- 8tbsp (120ml) olive oil
- Salt & freshly ground pepper as desired
- 2tsp (10ml) dried herbes de Provence (Provençal herbs)
- 8 wooden skewers

#### For the herb sauce

- 6½oz (200g) sour cream
- 2tbsp (30ml) finely chopped parsley
- 2tsp (10ml) grated horseradish
- ½tbsp (8ml) lemon juice

### Method

1 Clean the mushrooms. Wash, trim, quarter and deseed the pepper, remove all the white inner membranes and cut them crossways into wide strips. Wash and trim the courgettes and cut into bite-sized pieces. Peel and quarter the onions. Wash and dry the tomatoes.

2 Wash the thyme and rosemary and dry. Strip the leaves from their stalks and chop finely. Mix together the olive oil, salt, pepper, herbes de Provence, thyme and rosemary. Reserve 2tbsp (30ml) of the seasoned oil. Put the vegetables, onions and mushrooms into a bowl and add the rest of the seasoned oil. Mix and marinate for about 1 hour.

3 Then thread the vegetables, onions and mushrooms alternately onto the skewers. Grill for about 12- 15 minutes, turning frequently and brushing the skewers with the rest of the seasoned oil.

4 For the herb sauce, mix all the ingredients.

Serve the skewered vegetables with herb sauce & baguette.

# Stuffed courgettes

## Serves 2

## Ingredients

- 5oz (150g) parboiled long-grain rice
- 16fl oz (500ml) vegetable stock
- 1tbsp (15ml) oil
- 2 spring onions
- 2 medium-sized courgettes [each weighing 9½-11oz (300-350g)]
- tsp (10ml) olive oil
- 3½oz (100g) tomatoes
- Salt as desired
- Freshly ground pepper as desired
- 1½oz (50g) grated parmesan
- 1½oz (50g) low-fat quark (curd cheese)
- 1 egg yolk
- 1tsp (5ml) dried oregano
- 1½oz (50g) sour cream (10% fat)
- 2tsp (10ml) tomato puree

## Method

1 Put the rice into a pan with 10fl oz (300ml) vegetable stock and bring to a boil. Cook very gently over a very low heat with a lid on the pan for 15-18 minutes, until 'al dente'. Meanwhile trim, wash and finely chop the spring onions.
2 Wash the courgettes, halve lengthways and scrape out the flesh with a spoon, leaving a ¼in (½cm) border.

3 Finely chop half of the courgette flesh and the rest could be used for another dish.
4 Heat 1tbsp (15ml) oil and sauté the spring onions and chopped courgette for 4 minutes. Wash, halve, deseed and finely dice the tomatoes.
5 Preheat the oven to 400°F (200°C-fan oven) 350°F(180°C). Put the rice and the cooked courgette mixture into a bowl. Add half of the parmesan, the diced tomatoes, quark and egg yolk and mix well. Season the stuffing well with salt, pepper and oregano.
6 Season the courgette halves inside with salt and pepper and fill with the rice mixture. Place in a shallow baking dish. Pour 6½fl oz (200ml) of the vegetable stock into the dish. Sprinkle the stuffed courgettes with the rest of the cheese and 2tsp (10ml) olive oil and bake in the preheated oven for about 25-30 minutes.
7 Take the stuffed courgettes out of the oven and put onto plates. Mix the cooking liquid with the sour cream and tomato puree and serve with the courgettes. Serve with the rest of the hot rice. A green salad goes well with this dish.

# Peasant's salad with herb sheep's cheese and basil

Serves 4

## Ingredients

- ½cucumber
- 12½oz (400g) tomatoes
- 9½oz (300g) (herb) sheep's cheese
- ½ bunch spring onions
- 3tbsp (45ml) lemon juice
- 6tbsp (90ml) olive oil
- Salt & freshly ground pepper as desired
- A few basil leaves

## Method

1 Wash the tomatoes and cut into wedges.

2 Wash and trim the spring onions and cut into rings.

3 Wash the cucumber and cut into pieces. Dice the sheep's cheese.

4 Make a dressing from the lemon juice, oil, salt and pepper, check the seasoning and add to the salad ingredients. Mix well. Serve garnished with basil.

# Dandelion salad with bacon and croutons

## Serves 4

## Ingredients

- 1 clove garlic
- 4tbsp (60ml) olive oil
- 1tbsp (15ml) lemon juice
- 1tsp (5ml) Dijon mustard
- Salt as desired
- Freshly ground pepper as desired
- 4 rashers bacon (streaky)
- 1½oz (50g) white bread (crusts removed)
- 8oz (250g) dandelion leaves

## Method

1 Peel the garlic and chop very finely. For the vinaigrette, mix the garlic, 3tbsp (45ml) olive oil, lemon juice and mustard. Season with salt and pepper.

2 Fry the bacon in a dry frying pan until crisp, then drain on absorbent paper.

3 Cut the bread into ½in (1cm) cubes. Heat 1tbsp (15ml) oil in a frying pan and fry the bread until crisp and brown. Wash the dandelion leaves, dry and toss with the vinaigrette. Serve garnished with bacon and croutons.

# Chicken and rice soup
## Serves 4

### Ingredients

- 2 onions
- 1 clove garlic
- 2 carrots
- 2 sticks celery
- 1 cleaned boiling fowl, weighing approx. 38oz (1.2 kg)
- 1 bay leaf
- Salt & freshly ground pepper as desired
- 3½oz (100g) short-grain rice
- 2 eggs
- Juice of 1 lemon

### Method

1 Peel the onions, garlic and carrot, trim the celery and finely dice all the vegetables.

2 Wash the boiling fowl under cold, running water and put into a large pan. Add enough water to completely cover the chicken. Bring to a boil, skimming off the scum from time to time.

3 Add the diced vegetables and the bay leaf and season with salt and pepper. Return to a boil, cover with a lid and simmer for about 1½ hours, until the meat is soft. Drain through a strainer and reserve the broth.

4 Put the rice into the broth and cook according to the instructions on the packet.

5 Separate the meat from the bones, cut into bite-sized pieces and return to the broth. Season with salt and pepper. Remove the soup from the heat.

6 Whisk the eggs and mix smoothly with the lemon juice. Gradually stir in 1-2 ladlefuls of the broth. Then beat the egg, lemon and broth mixture into the soup. Do not let it boil or the soup will curdle. Season again with salt and pepper and serve immediately.

# Tuna and chick-pea salad
## Serves 4

## Ingredients

- 12½oz (400g) chick-peas
- Salt as desired
- 4 spring onions
- 1 stick celery
- 19oz (600g) tuna
- Freshly ground pepper
- 3fl oz (100ml) olive oil
- Juice and grated rind of 1 lemon
- 2tbsp (30ml) chopped parsley
- 1tbsp (15ml) chopped dill tips
- 1 clove garlic

## Method

1 Soak the chick-peas in cold water overnight, then drain, rinse and put into a pan. Cover with cold water and add salt. Bring to a boil, then turn down the heat and cook over a low heat for about 1 hour until the chick-peas are 'al dente'.
2 Trim the spring onions and celery. Cut the spring onions, including the pale green parts, into thin rings and slice the celery.
3 Rinse the tuna and pat dry. Slice and season both sides with salt and pepper.
4 Heat the olive oil in a frying pan and quickly sauté the fish on both sides. Deglaze with lemon juice and cook until done. Break up with a fork or dice and put into a bowl. Drain the chick-peas and add to the tuna. Add the spring onions, celery, lemon rind, parsley and dill. Peel and press the garlic and add to the salad. Season with salt and pepper and mix well.
5 Cover the bowl with cling film and put into the refrigerator for 3-4 hours. Stir once more, check the seasoning and serve.

# Fish soup with shrimps and vegetables

## Serves 2

## Ingredients

- 19oz (600g) fish fillets (e.g. cod, mackerel, seabass, turbot)
- Juice of 1 lemon
- 8oz (250g) potatoes
- 5½oz (175g) carrots
- 2 onions
- 8oz (250g) peeled tomatoes (canned)
- 2 sticks celery
- 1 clove garlic
- ½ bunch parsley
- 6tbsp (90ml) olive oil
- 1 bay leaf
- Salt & freshly ground pepper as desired
- 6½oz (200g) cooked shrimps or prawns

## Method

1 Wash the fish fillets under cold, running water, then pat dry and cut into portion-sized pieces. Put into a bowl, add 3tbsp (45ml) lemon juice, stir, cover and put into the refrigerator for about 30 minutes.
2 Peel and dice the carrots, potatoes and onions. Roughly dice the tomatoes. Wash, dry and slice the celery. Peel and press the garlic. Wash the parsley, dry and chop finely.
3 Heat the olive oil in a large pan and quickly sauté the potatoes, carrots and onions. Add the tomatoes, celery, garlic, parsley and bay leaf. Cover with water and season with salt and pepper. Cover with a lid and simmer the vegetables over a low heat for about 30 minutes.
4 Add the fish fillets and the marinade and simmer with the lid on for about 15 minutes. Add more water if necessary. When the fish is cooked add the shrimps and briefly bring to a boil. Season the soup to taste with salt, pepper and the rest of the lemon juice. Serve immediately.

# Vegetable soup with egg
## Serves 4

## Ingredients

- 6½oz (200g) leeks
- 6½oz (200g) carrots
- 12½oz (400g) potatoes, firm-cooking
- ½oz (20g) butter
- 2½oz (80g) onion
- 38fl oz (1.2 litres) beef stock
- 1tbsp (15ml) finely chopped marjoram
- Salt as desired
- Freshly ground pepper as desired
- 3½oz (100g) raw, smoked, streaky bacon
- 2 eggs
- Marjoram leaves to garnish

## Method

1 Remove the roots and some of the dark green parts from the leeks. Wash the leeks thoroughly, removing all the grit from between the leaves. Drain and slice thinly into rings. Peel the carrots and potatoes and cut both into slices approximately ⅛in (4mm) thick. Peel and finely dice the onions.

2 Melt the butter in a large pan, add the onions and sauté until translucent. Add the leeks, carrots and potatoes and sauté briefly. Add the stock. Season with marjoram, salt and pepper, bring to a boil, then reduce the heat and simmer over a low heat for 15-20 minutes.

3 Finely dice the bacon and fry in a dry frying pan until the fat runs. Add to the soup.

4 Whisk the eggs and stir into the soup. Heat until the egg sets. Ladle the soup into plates and garnish with marjoram.

# Greek salad

## Serves 4

### Ingredients

- 2 onions
- 5tbsp (75ml) black olives
- 6½oz (200g) feta cheese, cut into small pieces
- 4 tomatoes
- ½ iceberg lettuce
- Salt as desired
- Freshly ground pepper as desired
- 5tbsp (75ml) olive oil, cold pressed
- 1 cucumber
- 1 green pepper
- Fresh parsley
- Lemon juice

### Method

1 Peel the onions and cut into rings. Wash and quarter the tomatoes. Wash the lettuce and tear into bite-sized pieces. Peel and slice the cucumber. Wash, halve and deseed the pepper and cut into strips.

2 Mix all the ingredients with salt, plenty of pepper and 5tbsp (75ml) olive oil. Sprinkle with lemon juice to taste and serve garnished with fresh parsley leaves. Freshly baked flatbread goes well with this dish.

# Stuffed leg of lamb with aubergine and tzatziki

Serves 6

## Ingredients

- 1 medium-sized aubergine, sliced lengthways
- 2-3tbsp (30-45ml) olive oil
- 1 boned leg of lamb
- 2tbsp (30ml) dried oregano
- Salt & freshly ground pepper as desired

### For the paste

- 2tbsp (30ml) grated orange peel
- 1tsp (5ml) grated lemon peel
- 2tbsp (30ml) chopped sage leaves
- 2tbsp (30ml) chopped garlic cloves
- 2tbsp (30ml) chopped anchovies
- 1tsp (5ml) coarsely ground pepper
- 2tbsp (30ml) olive oil

### For the lemon tzatziki

- 14oz (450g) Greek yoghurt
- 1 cucumber, halved, deseeded and grated
- 1 bunch spring onions, chopped
- 2 cloves garlic, chopped
- 1 red chilli, chopped
- Juice of a lemon

### To serve

- 1tbsp (15ml) chopped dill tips

## Method

1 Brush the aubergine slices with oil and lightly brown on both sides in a frying pan. Set aside.

2 For the paste, combine all the paste ingredients and puree.

3 Spread the paste on the inside of the meat, lay the aubergine slices on top and roll up. Tie with kitchen string and leave in a cool place overnight. Weigh the joint. Rub the meat with oregano, salt and pepper.

4 Heat 2-3tbsp (30-45ml) olive oil in a flameproof roasting dish and quickly brown the meat on all sides. Then put into a preheated oven [400°F (200°C)] and roast for 15 minutes per 16oz (500g) + 15 minutes. Cover with aluminium foil for the first 30 minutes.

4 When done, take out of the oven, cover with aluminium foil and leave to rest for about 15–20 minutes.

5 For the tzatziki, squeeze out the grated cucumber and mix with the other ingredients. Put into a bowl and sprinkle with dill.

6 Serve the meat with the lemon tzatziki.

# Fried redfish fillet with skordalia
## Serves 4

### Ingredients

- 12½oz (400g) floury potatoes
- Salt as desired
- 2 cloves garlic
- 6tbsp (90ml) olive oil
- Juice of 2 lemons
- Freshly ground pepper
- 4 redfish fillets, each weighing 3½oz (100g) (alternatively zander or hake, unskinned fish can also be used)

### Method

1 Peel and dice the potatoes and cook in salted water for about 10 minutes. Drain and mash. Peel the garlic and press into the mashed potatoes. Add 4tbsp (60ml) olive oil and the juice of 1 lemon and season with salt and pepper.

2 Sprinkle the fish fillets on both sides with the remaining lemon juice and season with salt and pepper. Fry the fillets in 2tbsp (30ml) olive oil for 2-3 minutes each side. Serve with the Greek potato and garlic paste.

# Meatballs with tomatoes and olives

## Serves 4

## Ingredients

### For the meatballs

- 16oz (500g) minced lamb
- 1 shallot, finely chopped
- 2 stale bread rolls
- A little milk for soaking
- 1 egg
- 2tbsp (30ml) chopped parsley
- ½tsp (2½ml) salt
- Freshly ground pepper as desired
- Clarified butter

### For the tomato sauce

- 32oz (1 kg) ripe tomatoes
- 2 shallots
- 2 cloves garlic
- 3tbsp (45ml) olive oil
- 1tbsp (15ml) tomato puree
- 2 sprigs thyme
- Finely chopped basil leaves
- 2½oz (70g) green olives
- Salt as desired
- Pepper as desired

## Method

### For the meatballs

1 Sauté the shallots in butter until translucent. Soak the bread rolls in milk, then squeeze out and add to the minced lamb with the shallots and the egg. Add the parsley, season with salt and pepper and mix well. With wet hands form into small balls and fry on all sides in clarified butter until golden brown.

### For the tomato sauce

1 Make a slit in each tomato, scald in boiling water, then skin. Dice the flesh, removing the seeds and stalk scars.
2 Peel and dice the shallots. Peel & crush the garlic and sauté both in olive oil. Add the tomato puree and sauté for 3-4 minutes. Wash the herbs.
3 Add the tomatoes and one sprig of thyme to the shallots and simmer for about 30 minutes, stirring occasionally, until quite thick.
4 Add the finely chopped basil leaves and the rest of the thyme leaves, season with salt and pepper and stir in the olives.

Serve the meatballs in the tomato sauce.

# Tagliatelle with tomato and shellfish sauce

## Serves 4

## Ingredients

- 9½oz (300g) tagliatelle
- 12½oz (400g) each of mussels and clams, scrubbed well
- 3fl oz (100ml) white wine
- 2 cloves garlic
- 1 onion
- Salt as desired
- Freshly ground pepper as desired
- 11½oz (360g) canned tomatoes
- 3tbsp (45ml) chopped parsley

## Method

1 Peel and chop the garlic. Peel the onion and cut into thin strips.
2 Cook the tagliatelle in plenty of boiling, salted water.
3 Simmer the shellfish in a closed pan with the wine, garlic and onion, shaking the pan from time to time. Discard any mussels or clams that do not open.
4 Drain and chop the tomatoes and add to the shellfish. Cook over a fairly high heat for 2 minutes. Season with salt and pepper and mix in the parsley. Drain the pasta and add to the sauce. Mix well and serve.

# Deep-fried squid
## Serves 4

### Ingredients

- 16oz (500g) small squid (cleaned and prepared)
- Flour
- 2 eggs
- Salt as desired
- 16fl oz (500ml) vegetable oil
- 4 lemons, halved

### Method

1 Cut the squid into thick rings, or cut in half. Beat the eggs and salt lightly. Dip the squid rings first in flour, then in egg and then in flour again.

2 Heat the oil (it is hot enough when bubbles form on a wooden stick or the handle of a wooden spoon held in the oil) and deep-fry the squid rings, a few at a time. Serve immediately with the lemon halves.

# Lamb chops with ratatouille
## Serves 4

## Ingredients

- 4 lamb chops [each weighing about 2oz (60g)]

For the marinade
- 2 spring onions
- 2 cloves garlic
- 2 red chillies
- 4tbsp (60ml) olive oil
- 3tbsp (45ml) lemon juice
- 2tsp (10ml) grated lemon peel
- 1 bay leaf
- 1tbsp (15ml) rosemary
- 1tbsp (15ml) thyme
- Salt as desired
- Freshly ground pepper as desired

For the ratatouille
- 6½oz (200g) red and green peppers
- 5oz (150g)  baby aubergines
- 2½oz (80g) onions
- 2 cloves garlic
- 3½oz (100g) green beans
- 2 chillies
- 6½oz (200g) yellow plum tomatoes
- 3tbsp (45ml) olive oil
- Salt as desired
- Freshly ground pepper as desired
- 3fl oz (100ml) vegetable stock
- 3fl oz (100ml) sieved tomatoes
- 1tbsp (15ml) chopped herbs (parsley, thyme, rosemary)

## Method

For the marinade

1 Trim and wash the spring onions and cut into 4in (10cm) lengths. Peel and finely chop the garlic. Wash the chillies. In a dish large enough to hold the lamb chops mix the oil, lemon juice, lemon peel, herbs and seasonings. Add the chops, the spring onions, garlic and chillies, cover and marinate in the refrigerator for 3-4 hours.

For the ratatouille

1 Cut the peppers into quarters, remove the seeds and membranes and cut the flesh into ¾x¾in (2x2cm) pieces. Remove the stalks from the aubergines and cut into 2–3 pieces, cutting at an angle. Peel and halve the onions and cut into strips. Peel and thinly slice the garlic.

2 Trim the green beans, blanch in boiling, salted water, refresh in cold water then drain thoroughly. Wash the chillies and cut into thin rings, removing the seeds. Scald and skin the tomatoes, remove the seeds and cut the flesh into ¾x¾in (2x2cm) pieces.

3 Heat the oil in a frying pan and sauté the onion and garlic. Add all the vegetables, including the chillies, and sauté for a few minutes. Season with salt and pepper and deglaze with the vegetable stock. Stir in the strained tomatoes and the herbs. Reduce the heat and cook the vegetables for about 6-8 minutes.

For the meat, heat a frying pan and quickly fry the marinated chops on both sides. Add the vegetables from the marinade and briefly fry all together. Serve the chops with the ratatouille.

# German Shoemaker's pot

## Serves 4

### Ingredients

- 32oz (1 kg) potatoes
- 12½oz (400g) cooking pears
- 19oz (600g) lean pork belly
- 1tsp (5ml) caraway
- 1tbsp (15ml) finely chopped fresh mugwort (Artemisia vulgaris)
- Salt & freshly ground pepper as desired
- Meat stock

### Method

1 Wash the potatoes and peel the potatoes and the pears. Slice the potatoes. Quarter the pears and remove the cores. Cut the pork belly into ¾in (1.5cm) pieces.

2 Take a suitably sized flameproof roasting dish with a lid and put in half of the potatoes, then half of the pork belly. Next, lay the pears on top of the meat and cover with the remaining pork. Season with salt, pepper, caraway and mugwort. Finish with a neat, overlapping layer of potatoes. Season with salt and pepper and add enough stock just to cover everything.

3 Cook on the hob for 30 minutes with the lid on. Then put the roasting dish into a preheated oven [450°F (220°C)] without the lid and cook until the potatoes are nice and crisp, brushing with melted butter (optional).

# Boiled beef with root vegetables

## Serves 4

## Ingredients

- 32oz (1 kg) beef suitable for boiling, e.g. brisket or rump
- 1 bunch soup vegetables (carrots, leeks, Hamburg parsley (parsley root), celeriac)
- 80fl oz (2½ litres) water
- Salt as desired
- 5 crushed black peppercorns
- 3 parsley stalks
- 1 onion, unpeeled
- 1 onion, peeled and studded with 1 bay leaf and 2 cloves

### In addition

- 3½oz (100g) carrots
- 3½oz (100g) leeks
- 2½oz (80g) celeriac
- 1½oz (50g) Hamburg parsley
- 3½oz (100g) onions, cut into rings
- 1oz (30g) butter
- Salt as desired
- ½tsp (2½ml) paprika, sweet
- 1-2tbsp (15-30ml) white wine vinegar
- 1tbsp (15ml) chopped parsley
- ½oz (20g) freshly grated horseradish

## Method

1 Prepare the soup vegetables and chop roughly. Halve the unpeeled onion and brown on the hotplate, cut side down, until both halves are dark brown. Remove the peel.

2 Put 80fl oz (2½ litres) water into a pan with 1tsp (5ml) salt and bring to a boil. Add the meat, peppercorns, parsley stalks, studded onion, browned onion and the soup vegetables, cover with a lid and simmer over a low heat for 1½ hours, skimming off the scum from time to time.

3 Cut the carrots, leeks, Hamburg parsley and celeriac into julienne sticks.

4 When the meat is cooked, take it out of the broth, and keep warm in a little of the strained broth. Cook the vegetables in the rest of the strained broth until 'al dente'.

5 Heat the butter in a frying pan. Add the onion rings and sauté until soft. Season lightly with salt, paprika and deglaze with vinegar. Slice the meat and serve on a platter with the julienne vegetables, the horseradish and the onions. Add a little of the broth and sprinkle with parsley.

# Puff pastry cases filled with seafood and asparagus

## Serves 4

## Ingredients

- 12½oz (400g) puff pastry (frozen)
- 4 scallops, removed from their shells
- 5oz (150g) prawns, peeled and cleaned
- 16oz (500g) clams
- 32oz (1 kg) mussels
- 16oz (500g) green asparagus (1 bunch)
- 1 bunch spring onions
- 1½oz (50g) butter
- 13fl oz (400ml) cream
- 1 egg yolk
- Salt as desired
- Freshly ground pepper as desired

## Method

1 Preheat the oven to 400°F (200°C). Lay the puff pastry sheets on top of each other in twos and cut into 2 squares. Leave to thaw slightly and cut a small square out of each square (only cutting through the top layer). Beat the egg yolk with 1-2tbsp (15-30ml) water and brush the top layer of the pastries (the cut layer). Place on a baking tray lined with baking parchment and bake in the hot oven for 20 minutes until golden brown.

2 Clean the mussels in water and rinse under cold running water. Throw away any opened or broken mussels. Drain the remaining mussels in a sieve. Put the mussels into a large pan, cover with a lid and cook over a high heat, until they have opened. Discard any that have not opened. Take the mussels out of their shells, reserving the cooking liquid and put the mussel shells aside.

3 Cut the scallops into pieces. Heat 1tbsp (15ml) oil in a frying pan and fry the scallops over a high heat for 20 minutes until golden.

4 Wash the asparagus, cut off the woody ends and cut the spears into ¾in (2cm) lengths. Blanch in boiling, salted water for about 5 minutes. Drain.

5 Peel the spring onions and cut into 4 pieces, removing the green parts. Heat 1oz (30g) butter in a frying pan and gently fry the onion quarters. Add the asparagus and fry for a couple of minutes. Season with salt and pepper, cover with a lid and simmer for about 15 minutes.

6 Strain the reserved cooking liquid through a sieve into a pan and bring to a boil with the cream. Cook until the sauce thickens. Add the mussels, scallops, prawns and the contents of the asparagus pan and simmer over a low heat for 5 minutes.

7 Carefully lift off the puff pastry lids and fill the pastry cases with the sauce. Put the lids back on and serve immediately.

# Penne with tomato sauce and lentil sprouts
## Serves 4

## Ingredients

- Sprouts from 1½oz (50g) lentils (mountain lentils)
- 2 spring onions
- 1 clove garlic
- 2tbsp (30ml) olive oil
- 1 stick celery
- 6½oz (200g) diced tomatoes
- 3fl oz (100ml) water
- 3fl oz (100ml) white wine
- 2tsp (10ml) cane sugar
- Freshly ground pepper
- Sea salt as desired
- 2tbsp (30ml) balsamic vinegar
- 12½oz (400g) penne
- 1½oz (50g) freshly grated parmesan

## Method

1 Wash the spring onions and cut into thin rings. Peel and finely chop the garlic and sauté in olive oil with the spring onions.

2 Thinly slice the celery, add to the spring onions and garlic and fry gently all together for a couple of minutes. Add the tomatoes, water and white wine, cover with a lid and simmer for 30 minutes. 5 minutes before the end of cooking time, add the lentil sprouts and a little more water, if necessary. Season with sugar, pepper, salt and balsamic vinegar.

3 Cook the pasta according to the instructions on the packet, drain and mix with the lentil sprout and tomato sauce. Serve onto plates and sprinkle with parmesan. Serve immediately.

# Poached apricots with Farigoule (thyme liqueur)

Serves 4

## Ingredients

- 12 large ripe apricots
- 4tbsp (60ml) sugar
- 6½fl oz (200ml) water
- 3tbsp (45ml) icing sugar
- Farigoule (French thyme liqueur)
- 4tbsp (60ml) toasted flaked almonds

## Method

**1** Wash the apricots. Make a small cut in the end of each apricot and carefully pull out the stone (this only works if the apricots are really ripe).

**2** Put 6½fl oz (200ml) water and 4tbsp (60ml) sugar into a pan and bring to a boil, reduce the heat and add the apricots. Cover with a lid and poach over a low heat for about 6-7 minutes. Lift out with a slotted spoon or skimmer and drain.

**3** Caramelise the icing sugar in a frying pan over a low heat. Add the apricots and turn to coat all over.

**4** Serve the apricots into small bowls and sprinkle with the caramel and 3tbsp (45ml) ice-cold Farigoule. Serve garnished with toasted flaked almonds.

# Babas with cream and fresh strawberries

[For 6 dariole or baba moulds 3½oz (9cm) in diameter]

## Ingredients

- ½oz (20g) fresh yeast
- 1½fl oz (50ml) lukewarm milk
- 5½oz (175g) flour (white wheat flour)
- Salt as desired
- 1½oz (50g) softened butter
- 1tsp (5ml) sugar
- 2 eggs
- Butter for the moulds

### For soaking

- 6½oz (200g) sugar
- 13fl oz (400ml) strong coffee
- 2fl oz (60ml) rum

## Method

**1** Dissolve the yeast in the warm milk. Put the flour and salt into a bowl, mix in the yeast mixture and leave to rise for 15 minutes. Add the butter, sugar and eggs, knead well and leave to rise for a further 15 minutes.

**2** Preheat the oven to [400°F (200°C)] fan oven 350°F (180°C). Butter the moulds, half fill with the mixture and bake in the preheated oven for 12-18 minutes, depending on the size of the moulds.

**3** Put the sugar and coffee into a pan and boil to make a syrup. Add the rum and leave to cool. Take the babas out of the moulds and soak with the syrup while still warm. Serve with fresh fruit and whipped cream.

# Conversion guide

The Conversion guide given below is not an exact equivalent but an approximation, to make your measuring easier.

## Dry Measures

| Imperial | Metric |
| --- | --- |
| ½oz | 15g |
| 1oz | 30g |
| 2oz | 60g |
| 3oz | 90g |
| 4oz (¼lb) | 125g |
| 5oz | 155g |
| 6oz | 185g |
| 7oz | 220g |
| 8oz (½lb) | 250g |
| 9oz | 280g |
| 10oz | 315g |
| 11oz | 345g |
| 12oz (¾lb) | 375g |
| 13oz | 410g |
| 14oz | 440g |
| 15oz | 470g |
| 16oz (1 lb) | 500g |
| 24oz (1½lb) | 750g |
| 32oz (2lb) | 1Kg |

## Liquid Measures

| Imperial | Metric |
| --- | --- |
| 1fluid oz | 30ml |
| 2fluid oz | 60ml |
| 3fluid oz | 100ml |
| 4fluid oz | 125ml |
| 5fluid oz (¼pint /1gill) | 150ml |
| 6fluid oz | 190ml |
| 8fluid oz | 250ml |
| 10fluid oz (½pint) | 300ml |
| 16fluid oz | 500ml |
| 20fluid oz (1pint) | 600ml |
| 1¾pints | 1000ml (1 litre) |

# Conversion guide

| Imperial | Metric |
| --- | --- |
| ¼tsp | 1ml |
| ½tsp | 2½ml |
| 1tsp | 5ml |
| 1tbsp | 15ml |
| ¼cup | 60ml |
| ½cup | 125ml |
| 1cup | 250ml |

## Helpful Measures

| Imperial | Metric |
| --- | --- |
| ⅛in | 3mm |
| ¼in | 6mm |
| ½in | 1cm |
| ¾in | 2cm |
| 1in | 2.5cm |
| 2in | 5cm |
| 2½in | 6cm |
| 3in | 8cm |
| 4in | 10cm |
| 5in | 13cm |
| 6in | 15cm |
| 7in | 18cm |
| 8in | 20cm |
| 9in | 23cm |
| 10in | 25cm |
| 11in | 28cm |
| 12in | 30cm |

## Oven temperatures

| | °F (Fahrenheit) | °C (Celsius) | Gas Mark |
| --- | --- | --- | --- |
| Very low | 250 | 120 | 1 |
| Low | 300 | 150 | 2 |
| Moderately low | 325 | 160 | 3 |
| Moderate | 350-375 | 180-190 | 4 |
| Moderately hot | 400-425 | 200-210 | 5 |
| Hot | 450-475 | 220-230 | 6 |
| Very hot | 500-525 | 240-250 | 7 |

# Glossary

**Al Dente** In cooking, the adjective al dente meaning 'to the bite' in Italian describes pasta and rice that has been cooked so as to be firm but not hard. "Al dente" describes vegetables that are cooked through but still offer resistance to the bite.

**Anchovy** is a small fish usually stored in olive oil or salt. Anchovies are sold for flavoring.

**Balsamic Vinegar** is an aromatic, aged type of vinegar traditionally manufactured in Modena, Italy, from the concentrated juice, or must, of white grapes. It is very dark brown in color and its flavor is rich, sweet, and complex.

**Basil** The green aromatic leaves of basil or sweet basil are used fresh and dried as flavorings or spices in sauces, stews, salad dressings, vegetables, poultry, and vinegar.

**Brisket** is a meat cut from the breast of an animal, typically a cow.

**Button mushrooms** are young unopened mushrooms.

**Caraway** or Persian cumin is a biennial plant and native to Europe and western Asia. They are used as a spice in breads especially rye bread.

**Celeriac** also known as 'celery root,' 'turnip-rooted celery' or 'knob celery' may be used raw or cooked and it has the celery flavor, so it is often used as a flavoring in soups and stews.

**Cherry tomato** is a spherical miniature tomato. The fruit is glossy red, or occasionally yellow, and typically eaten in salad.

**Courgettes** The zucchini has a delicate flavor and can be appreciated with little more than quick cooking with butter or olive oil, with or without fresh herbs. Zucchinis can be eaten raw, in a cold salad, as well as hot and barely cooked in hot salads.

**Dandelion** is a widely distributed weed of the daisy family, with a rosette of leaves, bright yellow flowers followed by globular heads of seeds with downy tufts, and stems containing a milky latex.

**Dariole** is a small, round metal mold in which an individual sweet or savory dish is cooked and served.

**Dill** The fernlike leaves of Dill are aromatic, and is said to be best when used fresh, as it loses its flavor rapidly if dried.

**Feta Cheese** A white salty Greek cheese made from the milk of ewes or goats.

**Greek yoghurt** is usually made from sheep's milk, although cow's milk is also common. It has strong flavour, it is rich in fat and thick in texture.

**Hake** is a large-headed elongated fish with long jaws and strong teeth. It is a valuable commercial food fish.

**Herbes De Provence** (Provençal herbs) is a mixture of rosemary, marjoram, basil, bay leaf, thyme, and sometimes lavender flowers and other herbs. The mixture can be added to foods before or during cooking or mixed with cooking oil prior to cooking so as to infuse the flavor into the cooked food. They are rarely added after cooking is complete.

**Iceberg lettuce** is a plant with crisp green leaves commonly used in salads.

**Leek** is a plant related to the onion, with flat overlapping leaves forming an elongated cylindrical bulb that together with the leaf is eaten as a vegetable.

**Lentils** are high-protein pulse that are dried and then soaked before eating.

**Marjoram** is an aromatic undershrub with sweet pine and citrus flavor.

**Mugwort** is a plant of the daisy family, with aromatic divided leaves that are dark green above and whitish below, naive to north temperate regions.

**Oregano** is an aromatic plant related to marjoram, with leaves that are used fresh or dried as a culinary herb.

**Paprika** is a powdered spice with a deep orange-red colour and mildly pungent flavor, made from dried and ground fruits of certain varieties of sweet pepper.

**Parsley** is used for its leaf in much the same way as coriander or cilantro, but has a milder flavor.

**Plum tomato** is an Italian variety that is shaped like plum, typically used in cooking rather than raw.

**Quark** (Curd cheese) is a fresh cheese made from pasteurized milk. It is soft, white and unaged, similar to cream cheese.

**Rosemary** The fresh and dried leaves are used frequently in traditional Mediterranean cuisine as a herb; they have a bitter, astringent taste, which complements oily foods, such as lamb and fish.

**Rump** is the hind part of the body of a mammal or the lower back of a bird.

**Sage** is an aromatic plant with grayish-green leaves that are used as a culinary herb, native to southern Europe and the Mediterranean.

**Sea Salt** Gourmands often believe sea salt to be superior to ordinary table salt in taste and texture, though one cannot always taste the difference when dissolved. In preparations where sea salt's coarser texture is retained, it can provide different feel.

**Shallots** are commonly used in Thailand and come in all sizes and colors, including purple. If shallots aren't available at your local grocery store or are too expensive, a good substitute would be a combination of white cooking onion and garlic.

**Skordalia** is a thick Greek sauce made by combining crushed garlic with a bulky base-which may be a purée of potatoes, walnuts, almonds, or liquid-soaked stale bread-and then beating in olive oil to make a smooth emulsion. Vinegar is often added.

**Tagliatelle** is a pasta in long ribbon.

**Thyme** is a perennial native to the Mediterranean and is a popular culinary herb used fresh or dried.

**White wine vinegar** is a pale, slightly pungent vinegar made from white wine. It is the base for many herb vinegars.

**Zander** is a species of fish. Zander are often called pike-perch as they resemble the pike with their elongated body and head, and the perch with their spiny dorsal fin.